IMAGES
of America

TAMPA
THE EARLY YEARS

Franklin Street is pictured in this view (looking north) before the installation of streetlights, c. 1907. The First National Bank is the four-story building on the left. The jewelry store in the foreground was purchased by W.H. Beckwith, who remodeled the shop to make it one of the finest in the South.

IMAGES
of America

TAMPA
THE EARLY YEARS

Robert J. Kaiser

ARCADIA
PUBLISHING

The beautiful Hillsborough River is fed by the Green Swamp northeast of Hillsborough County. The river meanders through northeastern Hillsborough County and flows into Tampa Bay in downtown Tampa, where it serves as a source of water for the city.

CONTENTS

achelberg & Co.'s
Cigar Factory,
Ybor City, Fla.

The Stachelberg & Company Cigar Factory is typical of the hundreds of cigar factories in Tampa, *c.* 1900. Factories like this were scattered throughout Ybor City and West Tampa and employed thousands of workers.

Acknowledgments

Although all the material contained herein comes entirely from my personal collection, I would not have been able to acquire it without the assistance of the members of the Sunshine Postcard Club and two very good friends who have since passed away, Lucy O'Brien and John Lowe. A personal note of thanks also goes to my family for their tolerance and patience over the last 40 years.

INTRODUCTION

Local history has always been fascinating. It's always amazing to see it repeat itself time and time again, not necessarily in the physical sense but in the philosophical sense. Much can be learned from it. History tells us where we came from, why things happened the way they did, and why the future brings us what it does!

Few areas of Florida have as rich and as colorful a history as we have here in the Tampa Bay area. If pictures are words magnified, then pictures are a story in and of themselves. The following pages are not only a pictorial history of early Tampa but also of the cultural, economic, and social development of this great city. Tampa is a potpourri of many ethnic backgrounds, and each culture likes to boast of their own contribution to the city's development. But it was a collection of many ethnic backgrounds that made Tampa the city we know today. No one group can take credit single-handedly for what Tampa has become; there have been significant contributions made by all. War, however, has had the most dramatic influence on Tampa's history from the start. In 1823 the U.S. Government established a military outpost called Ft. Brooke, two years after Florida became a territory of the United States. This is the present-day site of downtown Tampa. The fort, a stronghold for the continuing skirmishes with the local native tribes, prevailed through three wars with the Seminole Indians. During the Civil War, blockade running was common in spite of the Federal Navy's attempt to seal off Ft. Brooke and the small village of Tampa. The Spanish-American War brought more people to Tampa than any other event in Tampa's history. World War I and World War II brought about several shipyards that built and repair ships, and many of them are still in business today.

Intangibles like natural resources, a natural deep-water port, and Tampa's proximity to the Panama Canal didn't hurt the city's development, either. Henry B. Plant's railroad, the construction of the Tampa Bay Hotel, and Tampa's five "C's" (climate, cattle, citrus, cigars, and cheap labor), along with visionary pioneers, came together to develop the area. This book concentrates on early Tampa and its development into a small, bustling city, particularly during the pre-1920s era, when a small fishing community was transformed into a boom town that continues to thrive.

The chapters are structured to detail the city's early growth and development into a very multi-cultured cross section of populace that has endured and still prospers. Tampa is truly an international city; people have been drawn to Tampa from all over the world. The Spanish-American War alone funneled over 50, 000 troops through Tampa and opened the eyes of the country and the world to Tampa's potential. The cigar industry brought in thousands more on a permanent basis for the making of handmade Havana cigars. The rapid pace of the construction of factories, hotels, and commercial buildings in town encouraged skilled construction workers to relocate here as well. The lumber, cattle, railroad, citrus, and phosphate industries added even more demand for workers to come to the "Gem of Florida's Gulf Coast," Tampa!

TAMPA, Fla. Franklin Street, Looking North.

Shown here is a view of Franklin Street in downtown Tampa, looking north. Franklin Street is the main street than runs north and south through the center of town. The streetcar line went right down the middle of the street. Streetcars from all of the surrounding neighborhoods ended up on Franklin Street.

One

CITY STRUCTURES

Tampa's new city hall, a massive brick and granite building, is still in use today and is located at Lafayette Street (now John F. Kennedy Boulevard) and Florida Avenue. The hall was build in 1915 at a cost of $235,000. The ten-story structure has a two-story clock tower that was donated by W.H. Beckwith Jewelry Company and was named "Hortense."

Tampa, Fla. Hillsborough County Court House.

The county courthouse in downtown Tampa was located within a small park, with pleasant, tropical shrubbery, flower beds, and a huge Confederate monument. This beautiful public green, complete with a small band shell for weekend entertainment, was built in 1891.

Free Library, Tampa, Fla.

Through the efforts of Louise F. Dodge, the society editor of *The Tampa Tribune*, and Hugh C. McFarlane, Tampa secured a grant from the Carnegie Foundation for $50,000 to build two libraries (this one at Seventh Avenue and Franklin Street) and one in West Tampa. This library was completed in 1915, and the architect was Fred James.

The United States of America is proclaimed in broad, bold letters above the doorway of this post office. Evidently, Uncle Sam is proud of his building and so are the people of Tampa. The post office occupies the first and second floors of the building, which is located between Twiggs and Zack Streets at Florida Avenue and was completed in 1904.

The Florida State Board of Health laboratory was located at 1301 Florida Avenue on the north side of the city. At the time of this photograph, c. 1917, the board had extensive authority to monitor sewage, the water supply, hospitals (private and public), and even the sale of milk.

Located at Harrison and Morgan Streets and established in 1850, this is Tampa's first cemetery, c. 1907. This area was considered to be out in the "boondocks" and well north of the city. Most of the cemetery business was handled by Tampa's first undertaker, John T. Givens, a carpenter from South Carolina.

The Confederate Monument is being set on the southeast corner of Court House Square in downtown Tampa, at Franklin and Lafayette Streets. The Tampa chapter of the United Confederate Daughters dedicated this marble monument in 1911. The monument was moved to the present courthouse in the early 1960s.

This is the Curry Building, c. 1910. Located in downtown Tampa at 817 Franklin and Cass Streets, this five-story, red-brick building houses the Economical Drug Store and the W.J. Chambers Shoe Company. Next door, to the right, is the S.H. Kress Building.

In 1823 the U.S. government sent Col. George Mercer Brooke to establish a military outpost at the mouth of the Hillsborough River and Tampa Bay and to assist in securing peace with the Seminole Indians. The main garrison was a wooden, two-story structure called Ft. Brooke, and it was located approximately on the spot where the Tampa Bay Lightning now play hockey.

The original Hillsboro Hotel was a three-story, brick building and was run by J.L. Tallevast. In 1912 the Hillsboro was replaced by a modern, 320-room hotel, which became one of Tampa's best in the downtown area. This photo was taken *c.* 1908, when rooms cost only $1 a night.

The Bay View Hotel was built by a German beer and liquor wholesaler, Robert Mugge, who came to Tampa in 1884. Originally, the hotel was to be a warehouse, but Mugge changed his mind during the construction. The hotel was different from all the others of the day; Mugge described it as a cross between a YMCA and a ten-story barroom. The hotel boasted 125 rooms and a large, decorated lounge on every floor. It was located at 218 Jackson Street and managed by C.H. Jewett.

The First Savings & Trust Company was chartered on April 28, 1914, and opened on July 1, 1914. The bank's president was A.C. Clewis. Years later, in July of 1949, the name of the bank was changed to the Marine Bank & Trust Company. After Clewis's death, George B. Howell succeeded him as the new president of the bank.

The DeSoto Hotel was located at 701 Marion Street and was built in 1892–1893 by Walter Parker and Capt. R.F. Webb. The building was designed by architect J.A. Wood, the same architect used for the Hillsborough County Courthouse and the Tampa Bay Hotel. The DeSoto had 150 rooms and was one of the few hotels that was open year round.

Read the Tribune and think of Tampa

Three Buildings Owned by Tampa's Morning Paper

This is a 1915 view of the buildings of *The Tampa Morning Tribune*, located on the west side of the 500 block of Tampa Street. The *Tribune* was called *The Sunland Tribune* in 1876 but, in 1883, was renamed *The Tampa Tribune* while under the ownership of Thomas K. Spencer.

The Citizens Bank and Trust Co., Tampa, Fla.

The Citizens Bank & Trust Company was established in 1895. For many years, this ten-story, brick building could boast of being the "big bank" in the "big building." Construction was begun in 1912 and finished in 1913 at a cost of more than $600,000. The bank was one of Tampa's first "skyscrapers."

The First National Bank of Tampa, headed by John Stocton and T.C. Taliaferro, was built in 1896 and had a four-story marble front. One of the most attractive buildings in downtown Tampa, the bank was formerly known as the Bank of Tampa, but changed its name in 1886, soon after receiving its national charter. The Bank of Tampa was one of the first in the state of Florida to receive a national charter.

The W.H. Beckwith Jewelry Store, located at 410 Franklin Street in downtown Tampa, was one of the finest jewelry stores in the South. Beckwith was born and educated in Georgia before coming to Tampa, and he had a wide range of expertise, having worked as an automobile salesman, a realtor, an investor, and even a sawmill operator. The tower clock that is presently in use at the city hall was donated by Beckwith. This interior photo was taken in early 1912.

17

The Palace Drug Store was owned by Isaac Gardner and was located at 1002 East Scott Street and the corner of Central Avenue, north of downtown Tampa. The drugstore also had an adjoining lunch room and was a very popular hangout when it opened, c. 1920. The proprietor was Flora C. Hicks. The early phone number only had four digits: 2795.

The Exchange National Bank of Tampa, located in downtown Tampa at Franklin and Twiggs Streets, was organized in March 1894 and opened in April of the same year. John Trice was the bank's first president but stayed less than a year before leaving to start the Citizens Bank & Trust Company. Trice was succeeded by Eduardo Manrara. The bank was replaced by the one in this photo in 1922.

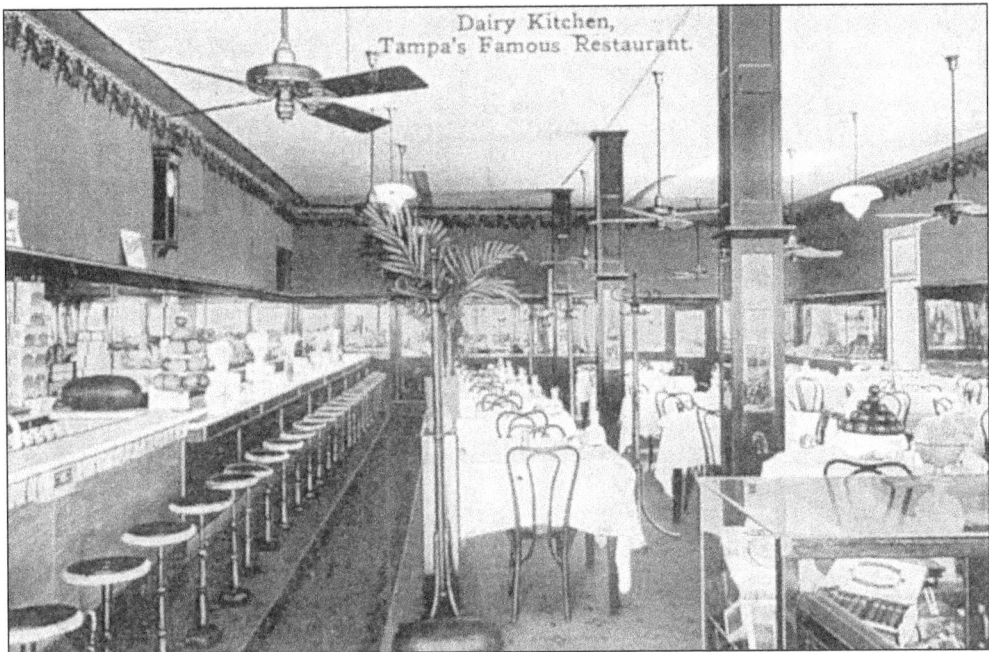

The Dairy Kitchen was owned by Nick Jack and specialized in dinners and business lunches. It was located at 201-203 East Lafayette and Tampa Street and was one of the most popular luncheon meeting places in town, c. 1920. It opened in 1900 and specialized in serving Tampa Bay oysters. This business also had only a four-digit phone number: 3065.

Taylor's Drug Store was located at 602 Franklin Street, at Twiggs Street. It was one of the first drugstores in Tampa and boasted "Perfection in Service" and a motto of "The Best Always." This rare interior photo dates from 1910. M.M. Taylor was the owner and liked to advertise that Kodak film was developed here for free.

The Olive Hotel (above) located in downtown Tampa, at Franklin and Washington Streets, was one of Tampa's finest hotels and eating establishments. After a ten-story addition was built, the name was changed to the Thomas Jefferson Hotel. In 1969 the hotel was demolished. Below is a rare view of the fine dining facilities, c. 1914.

Two

CITY STREETS

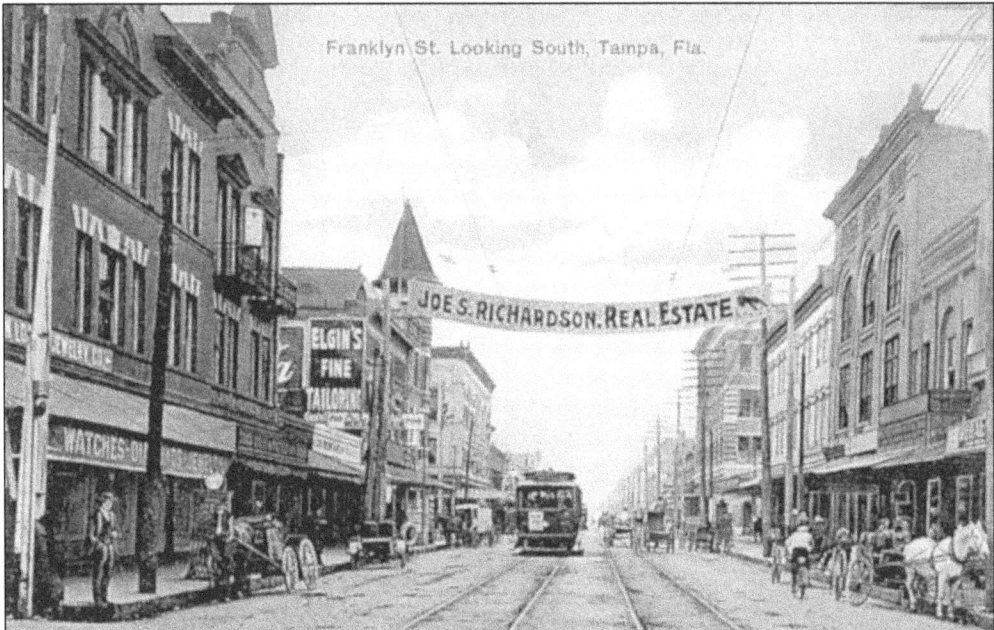

Notice the misspelling of "Franklyn" Street in this c. 1907 downtown view. The Joe S. Richardson real estate banner points towards the three-story, red-brick real estate offices before streetlights were installed. Railroad crossings were manually operated at left.

Looking north on Franklin Street around 1909, one can see the principal business thoroughfare of the "Magic City of the Gulf Coast." Tampa, which in addition to its reputation as a great winter resort, prides itself on being thoroughly metropolitan, offering in testimony handsome public and commercial buildings and every means of rapid transit.

This is Franklin Street, looking south, c. 1909. In addition to its superb hotels and winter resort status, Tampa points with pride to its excellent water systems, transit facilities, and well-paved streets.

This Franklin Street view, looking south, shows one of the first four-story buildings in Tampa, the First National Bank, as well as one of the very few streetlights in 1906.

Looking north on Franklin Street, one can see the Southern Hotel, the three-story building on the left at 1103 Franklin Street and one of the first hotels in downtown Tampa. Across Twiggs Street is Taylor's Drug Store, c. 1910.

This is a view of Lafayette Street in downtown Tampa looking west, c. 1906. The sign on the real estate building faces Franklin Street. This is one of the older buildings in Tampa and is known as "Tibbett's Corner" because it was once owned by the Tibbetts brothers who ran a confectionery shop there. Later, the building housed a much-frequented restaurant.

This is a 1906 view of Franklin Street, looking north from Lafayette Street, the busiest intersection in downtown Tampa. Transportation was mostly horse and buggy and Tampa Electric Trolleys during this time period. The building on the left is Giddens Clothing Company.

This c. 1905 bird's-eye view of the area around South Franklin Street shows that there were as many wooden buildings downtown as there were masonry ones. Except for a few steeples and domes, nothing was over three stories high.

Chartered on May 6, 1886, the First National Bank of Tampa is the oldest national bank in Florida. Originally organized in 1885 as the Bank of Tampa and located at Franklin and Washington Streets, the bank moved into the marble-faced structure seen here on the corner of Franklin and Madison Streets, next to Court Square Pharmacy, in 1896.

This is Twiggs Street, looking west, showing the Catholic Church of the Sacred Heart and the eight-story Hillsboro Hotel, c. 1915. Out of view to the right is the post office and the custom house.

Franklin Street is pictured here, looking south from Cass Street. Notice the Tampa Electric promotional banner draped across Franklin Street that reads "For a Brighter Tampa." The Economical Drug Store is to the left, on the corner.

This view, looking north on Franklin Street, shows the first home of the Citizens Bank & Trust Company at 701 Franklin Street. The three-story building opened on October 7, 1895, and the bank's first president was John Trice, who opened the bank with $100,000 in capital. Located next door was the Hale Drug Store, c. 1905.

Bird's Eye View, showing Post Office, Cathedral and Hillsboro Hotel, Tampa, Fla.

This bird's-eye view shows, from left to right, the post office/custom house, the Church of the Sacred Heart, and the Hillsboro Hotel. This 1914 view is looking towards the southeast.

This view of Franklin Street, looking south, shows Maas Brothers (left) and the American National Bank, formerly the Bank of Commerce in 1917 (right). This photo was taken c. 1919.

This is a view of Lafayette Street in downtown Tampa, looking west toward the Hillsborough River and the Tampa Bay Hotel. Only horse-drawn carriages and streetcars were used for transportation around 1907.

This bird's-eye view of downtown Tampa, c. 1915, shows one of the very few "skyscrapers" of the time, the ten-story Citizens Bank & Trust Company. In the foreground is Maas Brothers Department Store and Twomey's Millinery.

In this typical downtown Tampa view, looking north on Franklin Street from Lafayette Street, c. 1910, the Giddens Clothing Store is shown on the left. Notice that the streetcar's destination is the Mallory Docks at the mouth of Hillsborough River and Tampa Bay.

This aerial view of downtown Tampa shows Twiggs Street, looking west toward the Tampa Bay Hotel, c. 1910. The streetcar is on Franklin Street, in front of the Commercial Hotel. Diagonally across from each other are two competing drug stores; at left (by the streetcar) is Hutchinson-Cotter Drug Store, and at right (with a steeple) is the Taylor Drug Store.

Franklin Street, Looking North, Tampa, Fla.

This c. 1918 view from Twiggs Street, looking north on Franklin Street, shows the Taylor Drug Store in the left foreground and the Exchange National Bank of Tampa on the right.

Franklin Street is pictured here, c. 1915, looking north. At left is the Court Arcade, Beckwith Jewelry, and the First National Bank. Merchants used horse-drawn buggies for hauling deliveries.

This is a c. 1916 view of Florida Avenue, looking south. Shown from left to right are the post office, the Church of the Sacred Heart, the Elk's Home, and the Hillsboro Hotel.

The main business section of Tampa is pictured in this 1919 view looking south. On the horizon is Tampa Bay. The Hillsborough County Courthouse is in the middle of the photo and can be easily recognized by its Moorish architecture and ornate roof line.

Franklin Street looking south is pictured here, c. 1909, when the Wolf brothers established their clothing store in a building on the right side of the street. On the left are the Chicago Furniture House and the Tampa Hardware Company.

This is Florida Avenue, looking north from Polk Street c. 1904, in a very rare view of two early Tampa hotels, the Leport (left) and the Palmetto (right). The Palmetto Hotel was built in 1884 and was Tampa's leading hotel at the time, offering about 40 rooms. In this photograph, the fire-escape ladder on the side of the building is visible.

This 1914 bird's-eye view of downtown Tampa shows the Bank of Tampa, the Commercial Hotel, the Snow-Bryan Company (which distributed Checona Evans Ale, a non-intoxicating soft drink), the Hutchinson Drug Store, the Tampa Bay Hotel, the warehouse district, and Josiah Richard's sign hawking rare bargains on area property available and sporting signs which read, "on sale now!"

This is a great bird's-eye view of the Atlantic Coast Line Railroad loading warehouse area on the Hillsborough River in the western part of downtown Tampa. This *c.* 1910 view looking east was taken from one of the minarets of the Tampa Bay Hotel.

This is Franklin Street, looking south, *c.* 1910. The visible intersection is that of Franklin and Twiggs Streets. The Commercial Hotel (formerly the Southern Hotel) shares the corner with Taylor Drug Store.

Three

HYDE PARK

This is Henry B. Plant's home in East Point, Groton, Connecticut. This "Connecticut Yankee" never had a home in Tampa, but his vision for developing this small fishing village into a great city had an enormous effect on the area.

This picture from a pioneer postcard—one of the earliest Tampa postcard views known—was published prior to May 19, 1898. Cards of this vintage were either of expositions or were advertisements for famous cities or resorts, such as the Tampa Bay Hotel, shown here.

The Tampa Bay Hotel is located in Plant Park, across from downtown Tampa. The Hillsborough River flows just to its east and Hyde Park is to its south. Henry B. Plant built the hotel, which was opened to the public in 1889.

The Tampa Bay Hotel was built on the banks of the Hillsborough River. The largest hotel in Florida at the time, it was furnished with art and furniture from all over the world. The Moorish architecture made it unique; the cost of the building and the lavish interior decorations was over $3 million.

This is the parlor of the Tampa Bay Hotel. As can be seen here, H.B. Plant spared nothing in the hotel's decoration and furnishings. The Moorish and Oriental art work make the hotel unique and exquisite.

FLORIDA ASPHALT BLOCK PAVING COMPANY
TAMPA, FLORIDA

BOULEVARD
LAID 1912

One of Tampa's first highways was developed by Alfred R. Swan and Eugene Holtsinger. Prior to the development of Bayshore Boulevard, this area was nothing but mud flats and fiddler crabs. After a lengthy process of dredging and the construction of a seawall, the land was known as "Suburb Beautiful."

Bay Shore Boulevard, Tampa, Fla.

The developers of Bayshore Boulevard put aside expensive waterfront lots for the beautification of Tampa, and in 1914, Bayshore Boulevard was bricked at a cost of almost $90,000 for a little over 3 miles. Hence, the Bayshore district was born.

This *c.* 1909 bird's-eye view shows the new Hyde Park section of Tampa developed by O.H. Platt. The 20-acre plot of land was purchased from the estate of the Robert Jackson family. These 1/4-acre tracts went fast in 1886.

Although Hyde Park was desirable from the start, it wasn't until H.B. Plant promised to build the Tampa Bay Hotel that the area really began to flourish. The real estate company of Salomonson and Fassenden handled most of the sales in Hyde Park.

This is a very early view of Bayshore Boulevard. Notice the streetcar lines on the left that connect South Tampa to the downtown area. This section of Tampa has become a very exclusive and beautiful residential area overlooking the bay.

Where Hyde Park Avenue runs into Tampa Bay marks one of the oldest residential sections in Tampa. This area is within walking distance of downtown and is saturated with some of the most elegant homes in the city.

This view of Hyde Park Avenue looking north shows how the area appeared in 1905. At the north end of the avenue is the Tampa Bay Hotel and the exotic grounds that surround it.

This is a rooftop view of early Hyde Park looking north, c. 1907. The minarets of the Tampa Bay Hotel can be seen at the extreme right of the photo. Notice that there were even medians back then!

View on Plant Ave., Tampa, Fla.

Plant Avenue is another main street in Hyde Park, which is dotted with palms and oaks and inhabited by some of Tampa's most prominent citizens. This is a c. 1911 view.

This c. 1912 view is of Plant Avenue in Hyde Park, located just west of downtown Tampa. These trees now shade the entire street and the sidewalks.

Thoroughly modern and up to date, Tampa is the pride of Florida's west coast. This avenue in Hyde Park can hardly be rivaled in the older cities of the United States. The street is 80 feet wide and is located at the entrance to one of the most affluent neighborhoods in Tampa.

Hyde Park Avenue was the first street opened on the 20-acre tract of land that O.H. Platt developed in 1886. The first day of sales in the development totaled $2,225, and Judge Joseph B. Wall was one of the first buyers of the 1/4-acre lots. The neighborhood was named after Platt's hometown of Hyde Park, Illinois.

These private residences on Grand Central Avenue were typical of the architectural style of the early 1900s. The avenue starts at Lafayette Street and Magnolia Avenue and goes east. Today, Lafayette Street is called John F. Kennedy Boulevard.

This section of scenic Bay View Drive is the Bayshore Drive and Hyde Park area before it was converted to Bayshore Boulevard in 1914 and repaired in 1925 (after damage from a 1921 hurricane) at a cost of $400,000. In 1935, with a quarter-million dollars in aid from the Work Projects Administration added to city funds, Bayshore Boulevard was completed from the Platt Street Bridge to near Ballast Point at a cost of well over $1 million.

Bay Shore Boulevard, Tampa, Fla.

This view of Bayshore Boulevard is where Hyde Park meets the Tampa Bay. The streetcar tracks going to Ballast Point are in the foreground. The boulevard is lined with large mansions like the one shown in this view from 1906.

FLORIDA ASPHALT BLOCK PAVING COMPANY
TAMPA, FLORIDA

SO. DELAWARE AVENUE

This is a typical street scene in the Hyde Park area. The small trees pictured here are now massive oaks, providing shade for streets and lawns. Delaware Avenue starts at Bayshore Boulevard on the bay and goes north.

45

BIRDSEYE VIEW OF MOUTH OF HILSBORO RIVER, TAMPA, FLA.
(PHOTO TAKEN FROM SMOKESTACK 185 FEET HIGH

PUB. BY WM. S. OPPENHEIM

This bird's-eye view from Peter O. Knight Tampa Electric Power House's 185-foot smokestack shows how little was developed in Tampa around 1904. Shown at left in the bay is what was once known as Seddon Island, now called Harbor Island. At right in the bay is the present-day Davis Island, and in the middle is the mouth of the Hillsborough River.

BIRDSEYE VIEW, HYDE PARK, TAMPA, FLA.
(PHOTO TAKEN FROM SMOKESTACK 185 FEET HIGH

PUB. BY WM. S. OPPENHEIMER

This bird's-eye view of Hyde Park was taken from 185 feet up the same smokestack and prior to the development of Bayshore Boulevard, Davis Island, and modern bridges and streets. Notice the many outhouses in the foreground of this c. 1904 scene.

46

HYDE PARK AVENUE, TAMPA, FLA.

This 1905 aerial view of Hyde Park shows a thriving suburb within walking distance of downtown Tampa. On the horizon is the future Davis Island and Tampa Bay.

BIRD'S-EYE VIEW OF TAMPA FLORIDA, LOOKING SOUTHEAST FROM TAMPA BAY HOTEL.

In this c. 1905 view of Hyde Park looking southeast, the city of Tampa is to the upper left. Seddon Island is to the right, just off shore. This area is part of the original 20-acre Hyde Park tract.

47

Another view of Hyde Park shows the neighborhood's storm drainage system, c. 1909. Most of these two-story homes are still standing today. The neighborhood is just as prestigious today as it was at the beginning of the century but now has better storm drainage.

The red brick, two-story building in this c. 1912 view is Tampa Fire Department Station #3, located at the corner of Platt Street and Magnolia Avenue, in the Hyde Park section of town. Equipped with the latest fire trucks as well as reliable old horse-drawn wagons, the station opened for service in 1911. Mr. T.S. Leggett was the captain and Mr. J.E. Holton was lieutenant.

Four

WATERWAYS AND HIGHWAYS

On the Hillsborough River, looking north from the Tampa Bay, the minarets on the Tampa Bay Hotel can be seen on the horizon to the left. To the right is a small boat, *Mermaid of Tampa*, which was used for short excursions up and down the river.

Along the Docks, Tampa, Fla.

The *H.B. Plant* is docked at the Independent Line Steamer's Tampa Bay and Hillsborough River wharf in order to take on passengers for various Gulf Coast destinations, *c.* 1908. Notice the four-masted schooners double parked to the right.

Lafayette Street Bridge, Tampa, Fla.

WALK YOUR HORSES

The Lafayette Street Bridge, shown here looking west toward the Tampa Bay Hotel, crosses the Hillsborough River. Notice the sign that reads, "Walk Your Horses" under penalty of law!

This *c.* 1907 view of the Hillsborough River, looking south, was taken from the Lafayette Street Bridge. The Peter O. Knight Tampa Electric Power House is on the right, sporting its 185-foot smokestack.

LAFAYETTE STREET BRIDGE
TAMPA, FLA.

This is a view of the Lafayette Street Bridge, looking east, *c.* 1907. Steamer docks at right were used to transport people to St. Petersburg and Pass-a-Grille, which was part of Hillsborough County at the time this picture was taken. The pipe supports on the bridge helped support the electrical streetcar power lines overhead.

51

This aerial view of downtown Tampa was taken from one of the minarets on the Tampa Bay Hotel, c. 1907. The Hillsborough River, the warehouse district, and the railroad lines are in the foreground. The roof of the Tampa Bay Casino can also be seen.

The Tampa harbor, pictured from the Lafayette Street Bridge, looking south, shows the calm waters as the river meets the bay. On the right is the Tampa Electric Power House. On the left are docking facilities and the warehouse area, c. 1908.

This waterfront view shows the head of the beautiful Tampa Bay, the pride of Florida's west coast, at the mouth of the Hillsborough River, c. 1905. The deep-water terminal of the Plant System Railroad is located at Port Tampa, 9 miles down the bay.

An early view of the Tampa riverfront, c. 1906, shows the Hillsborough River as it flows into the Tampa Bay on the way to the Gulf of Mexico. At left is the western shoreline of downtown Tampa and the many docks that line the waterfront.

Tampa Bay Hotel, and Hillsboro River, Tampa, Fla.

In this c. 1906 view of downtown Tampa on the river, looking northwest, the minarets of the Tampa Bay Hotel are on the horizon. On the lower left is the dock for catching a boat to Sulphur Springs up river.

Looking East across Lafayette Street Bridge, Tampa, Fla.

Looking east across the Lafayette Street Bridge towards downtown, c. 1917, this photo shows all the forms of local transportation available at that time (streetcars, cars, bicycles, horse and buggies, and just plain walking).

54

The Mallory Docks with two U.S. gunboats at dock, c. 1911, are viewed here from the newly developed Seddon Island wharf. The dredged channel was first used by the Mallory Steamship Line, which gave rise to the name Mallory Channel.

An early 1904 view of the Hillsborough River in the downtown area shows, to the left, the Tampa Bay Hotel and Casino and, to the right, the old Lafayette Street Bridge. Notice the small boat, *Mermaid of Tampa*, on the right.

This is a harbor view of the Hillsborough River from the old Lafayette Street Bridge, looking towards the bay, c. 1905. Notice the new seawall under construction in the foreground. The Tampa Electric Power House is across the river, on the right.

This 1906 view looks east from Hyde Park toward downtown Tampa on Lafayette Street. Out of view at left is the Tampa Bay Hotel. The Magnolia Studios is the first building on the right. Overhead, at right, are the transmission lines from the powerhouse that supplied electrical power to the downtown area.

The Hillsborough River flows into the bay and skirts the downtown area. In the foreground is the Lafayette Street Bridge, connecting Hyde Park with downtown Tampa. This old, wooden bridge was replaced in 1914 by a steel and masonry structure.

This is Nebraska Avenue, c. 1907. One of the main north-south routes in Tampa, Nebraska connects Union Station to the south with all points north; it is also the main route to Sulphur Springs from Tampa.

The corner of Seventh Avenue and Morgan Street in Tampa Heights is north of downtown Tampa and west of Ybor City. It was part of an ideal residential area filled with many beautiful homes that still stand today. Notice that the street signs were nailed to trees in 1908.

This residential area with its lovely shaded streets was located west of Ybor City, c. 1909. The entire neighborhood had red-brick streets.

This is the residential section of western Seventh Avenue in Tampa Heights, c. 1911. The area is currently undergoing a major restoration of its architectural treasures and is the envy of surrounding neighborhoods.

Tampa Heights is located just north of the city of Tampa and west of Ybor City. Once a natural suburb of Tampa, the area was used as a military camp during the Spanish-American War in 1898. The camp was just one of the many that housed the thousands of troops that came through Tampa.

The Long Bridge over Six Mile Creek, Tampa, Fla.

2/2/59

Six Mile Creek, at the time of this picture, was a very small river that drained into Sparkman Bay, now known as McKay Bay. The creek is located 6 miles east of downtown Tampa.

Six Mile Creek, Tampa, Fla.

Six Mile Creek emptied into Sparkman Bay about one mile across from Palmetto Beach in South Tampa. When this picture was taken in 1909, fishing was great, but the area was considered far out in the country.

Five

TRANSPORTATION

The many excursion boats that frequented Tampa and the surrounding areas made regular trips between Bradenton, Sarasota, St. Petersburg, Tarpon Springs, Clearwater, and Tampa. This 1908 photo shows, clockwise from top left, *Manatee, Favorite, H.B. Plant,* and *Pokanoket.*

St. Petersburg from Tampa Bay, Fla.

The *H.B. Plant* steamer, seen here leaving St. Petersburg on the way to Tampa, was one of the fastest steamers cruising Tampa Bay. It was put into service by the Plant Steamship Company in 1900.

Steamer "H. B. Plant" at A.C.L. Dock. St. Petersburg, Fla.

The steamer *H.B. Plant* arrives at the Atlantic Coast Line Railroad dock in St. Petersburg. In March 1909, after a bitter price war over the cost of carrying passengers and cargo, a merger of companies resulted in the formation of the St. Petersburg Transportation Company headed by H. Walter Fuller. The new line was commonly known as the "Favorite Line."

62

The steamers *Favorite* and *Manatee* were part of the St. Petersburg Transportation Company, which also operated the *H.B. Plant*, *Terasia*, and *Vandalia*. These steamers serviced the entire Gulf Coast area daily.

This *c.* 1910 view shows one of the many boat landings along the Florida Gulf Coast at Anna Maria Beach in Manatee County. The steamer *Favorite* could carry 500 people for a day's outing. Smaller vessels are nearby to provide further "taxi service."

The steamer *Gypsy* was run by one of the smaller steamship lines operating in the bay area. *Gypsy* made regular stops in St. Petersburg, Pass-a-Grille, and Tampa. In fact, the line was called the Tampa-St. Pete-Pass-a-Grille Line.

THE "FAVORITE" AT DOCK BY MOONLIGHT ST. PETERSBURG, FLA.

The *Favorite* makes a moonlight trip from Tampa to St. Petersburg. She could hold over 500 passengers and was owned by the Tampa Bay Transportation Company at the time this photo was made. In 1906, this famous boat was bought in New York for $80,000.

New Lafayette Street Bridge, open, Tampa, Fla.

The new Lafayette Street Bridge was designed by Alexander Twombley of New York, and construction was done by Edwards Construction Company. The span was 80 feet wide. The bridge was completed in April 1913 at a cost of $240,000. Tampa Electric donated $50,000 to help pay for its construction.

Favorite Line Steamers at their dock, Tampa, Fla.

The Favorite Line steamers at their docks at the mouth of the Hillsborough River are *Pokanoket* (left) and *Favorite* (right). The commonly known "Favorite Line" was owned by Walter Fuller of St. Petersburg. The docks were at the foot of Jackson Street and the Hillsborough River.

S. S. Alamo and S. S. Lampasas at Mallory Line Dock, Tampa, Fla.

The SS *Alamo* and the SS *Lampasas* are docked at the Mallory Line docks. These steamers made regular runs to New York City, Key West, Mobile, and Philadelphia. The Mallory Line primarily handled freight but did accommodate a limited number of passengers. This photo is from *c.* 1910.

The Mallory Line, whose docks are seen here, was one of the first to bring large steamers to Tampa, making Tampa a regular port of call in 1908. After that, it only took about one year for the area become so congested that a major harbor development had to be undertaken.

One of the many Mallory Line steamships is seen here at dock in Tampa getting ready to take a load of freight to New York, c. 1912. Tampa's port at this time had become one of the busiest ports in the Southeast.

The Mallory Steamship Company docks were located at the foot of Franklin Street. Mallory was the first shipping line to use the newly dredged channel in 1905. This created a great demand for dock workers and laborers.

S. S. "Olivette," Cuba and Port Tampa Service.

The SS *Olivette* is shown here docking at Port Tampa. The H.B. Plant System owned the steamer and made regular runs between Tampa and Cuba. The *Olivette* was the second steamer used by the Plant System and was named after a comic opera.

TAMPA'S NEW FLOATING HOTEL
STEAMER "HARRY G. DREES"

BEAUTIFUL CABIN AND DINING SALON

Mississippi and Ohio Steamboat Co.

BRANCH OFFICE
115 WEST LAFAYETTE STREET
TAMPA, FLORIDA

GENERAL OFFICE
511 INTERNATIONAL LIFE BLDG.
ST. LOUIS, MO.

The steamer *Harry G. Drees* was a beautiful, floating hotel owned by the Mississippi and Ohio Steamship Company in St. Louis, Missouri. They had a Tampa office at 115 West Lafayette Street, across from the Tampa Bay Hotel and just north of the Lafayette Street Bridge, *c.* 1920.

The luxury steamer *Mascotte* was put into service on January 7, 1886, connecting Tampa with Cuba. When the Spanish-American War broke out, this 200-foot ship was sent to Cuba and loaded to capacity with tobacco to prevent shortages for the many cigar factories in Tampa. The ship has played such an important part of local history that it is presently on the official Seal of the City of Tampa.

This view of the Mallory docks shows how the facilities were expanded to handle the increase in shipping traffic between Tampa and New York, Mobile, and Key West. The downtown area is due north on Franklin Street.

Opening
St Petersburg-Tampa
Air Boat Line

Tony Jannus was the best pilot at the Benoist Aircraft Company of St. Louis, Missouri. He was sent to St. Petersburg to make the first commercial flight to Tampa as part of a publicity stunt. Jannus's passenger, A.C. Pheil of St. Petersburg, paid $400 for the honor of accompanying Jannus on the ride. The morning flight only took 23 minutes and was received by over 3,000 greeters in Tampa. Jannus's flight was only 50 feet above the bay.

Photo By Weimer

THE TAMPA MOTORLESS AND THE INVENTOR A. MEIRA

This aircraft was built in Tampa by A. Meira and was called the "Tampa Motorless." The inventor is seen here posing by the propeller in a picture taken by local photographer Weimer in the early 1900s. Needless to say, the vehicle wasn't successful.

National attention was focused on Tampa and St. Petersburg in 1914, with the formation of the St. Petersburg-Tampa Airboat Line by the Benoist Aircraft Company of St. Louis. Although the effort was not a financial success, the notoriety of being the world's-first commercial airline was quite an accomplishment.

This airship was part of the Florida State Fair festivities held on February 10, 1910. The fairgrounds were located adjacent to the Tampa Bay Hotel grounds and Plant Park to the north. The airship was a major attraction and one of the biggest highlights of the 1910 festival.

The brand-new Tampa Electric Company's streetcar barn was officially opened on February 14, 1912. The public was invited to tour the barn, which was located on the northwest corner of Seventh and Ola Avenues, by the Hillsborough River. It was open between 3:00 and 5:00 p.m. and managed by J.C. Woodsome.

This is one of the Tampa Electric Company's streetcars, with conductor A.J. Barnes pictured at right. The streetcar is at Thirty-first Street and Second Avenue in the South Gary section of East Tampa, c. 1915.

The Tampa Northern Railroad was the third railroad to come to Tampa and connected the city with Brooksville and Centralia in northwest Hernando County. The line was completed October 1, 1907. Peter O. Knight was instrumental in the acquisition of property for the railroad, which was merged with the Seaboard Airline Railroad on July 1, 1912. This gave the Seaboard Railroad more than 5 miles of waterfront and Seddon Island.

Tampa's Union Station, located on Nebraska Avenue and Cass Street, was completed on May 15, 1912. The Seaboard Airline Railroad and the Atlantic Coast Line Railroad built the depot through a united effort at a cost of $100,000. Peter O. Knight and *The Tampa Tribune* were also instrumental in the station's development. At the same time, the Southern Express Company erected its own building nearby.

73

TROOPS EMBARKING AT PORT TAMPA FOR SANTIAGO, CUBA.

Thousands of troops headed for Cuba during the Spanish-American War in the spring of 1898. Teddy Roosevelt and his famous Rough Riders of the period left a legacy to Tampa that is still enjoyed today.

This open-air roadster is parked on the west side of the Tampa Bay Hotel, and the driveway and parking area are in the process of being bricked in. This photo was taken c. 1915.

Six

COMMERCE AND
INDUSTRY

Tampa ships more phosphate than any other port in the world; the phosphate is transported by rail to Tampa's port for export. Phosphate mining in Florida was begun in 1888 by the Arcadia Phosphate Company, and since that time Florida has mined about half of all phosphate worldwide. This photo is from c. 1908.

This is a c. 1905 view of the docking facilities at Port Tampa. In the foreground is the famous tugboat *Neptune*, which serviced the port for many years. Steamers and schooners from all over the world were common visitors here.

This is one of the very early phosphate loading techniques used c. 1903 at Port Tampa's loading facilities. The product is being delivered by the Atlantic Coast Line Railroad, which acquired the Plant System and all their facilities on May 1, 1902.

Steamers from all over the world dock at Port Tampa and carry everything from crude oil to cattle. The natural deep-water port is one of the busiest along the Gulf Coast. In this *c.* 1910 image, the steamer in the slip is *Inverness*, a peculiar type of steamer called a "truck back."

The freighter *Tynedale* is being loaded with phosphate at the Seaboard Dock in Tampa, *c.* 1915. In 1889, a German homesteader named Albertus Bogt discovered rock phosphate in Marion County, Florida. News of the discovery spread like wildfire, and soon, Tampa became the principal shipping point for the world.

This picture is unique in that it shows a critical process in the manufacture of good Cuban cigars. The docks at Port Tampa, 9 miles south of the city, receive Cuban tobacco leaf on one side of the dock and warehouse. Then, the leaf is transferred to rail on the other side of the warehouse to be taken inland to the Sanchez & Haya Factory for further processing.

New factory of SANCHEZ & HAYA COMPANY, 14th Ave. and 17th St., makers of the Finest Havana Cigars, Factory No. 1, Tampa, Florida.

This modern factory of Sanchez & Haya Cigar Factory was located at Fourteenth Avenue and Seventeenth Street in Ybor City, and replaced an earlier wood-frame structure at Seventh Avenue and Fifteenth Street that was built in 1886. Sanchez & Haya was the first cigar factory to operate in Tampa and was, therefore, assigned the cherished title "Factory #1." Many more factories followed soon afterward.

This is a typical interior view of one the over 150 cigar factories in the Tampa area in the early 1900s. All the cigars were hand-made and were shipped all over the world. Notice that even little children were employed in the industry.

The M. Stachelburg & Company was founded by Michael Stachelburg in New York in 1857. After opening a successful branch in Ybor City at Seventh Street and Fourth Avenue, he moved his entire operation to the Tampa area. The factory employed 700 cigar makers in its three-story brick building.

The Samuel L. Davis Cigar Factory was located in West Tampa on Howard Avenue and was the proud home of the El Sidelo brand cigars. Samuel and his brother Fred owned two factories; Fred handled the one in New York and Sam handled the Tampa factory that was built in 1905.

This is the Havana-American Company, Seidenberg branch, which employed about 400 workers. One of the most attractive factories in Tampa, the building had adjoining gardens that required a full-time landscaper and gardener year round.

The Pendas & Alvarez Cigar Company was the home of the Daniel Webster brand, and the company's cigars are known and sought after wherever men have learned what clear Havana means. The Pendas & Alvarez factory building was one of the finest ever constructed, with three stories of red brick, a basement, and a seven-story clock structure at the main entrance.

The Berriman Brothers Cigar Factory was located at 2311 Eighteenth Street, though the company's headquarters were in Chicago. Their Tampa factory was a very attractive three-story building with a full basement.

Tampa is the center of the citrus fruit territory in this part of Florida and annually ships thousands of boxes of grapefruit and oranges to markets all over the world. The Florida Citrus Exchange is also located in Tampa. At the time of this 1909 photo, the average box of citrus cost $1.34.

In the early 1900s through the 1920s, celery was one of the largest agricultural crops in Hillsborough County. It was so popular that even a soft drink was made from it called "Cello."

Farming in Tampa is a 12-month-a-year business. Some of the most fertile land in Florida lies in Hillsborough County. This is a c. 1914 view of a typical crop going to market.

The Tampa Bay and surrounding waters are an abundant source of a variety of seafood, including mackerel, trout, kingfish, grouper, redfish, snapper, and tarpon (a sportsman's real challenge and trophy to all that land one).

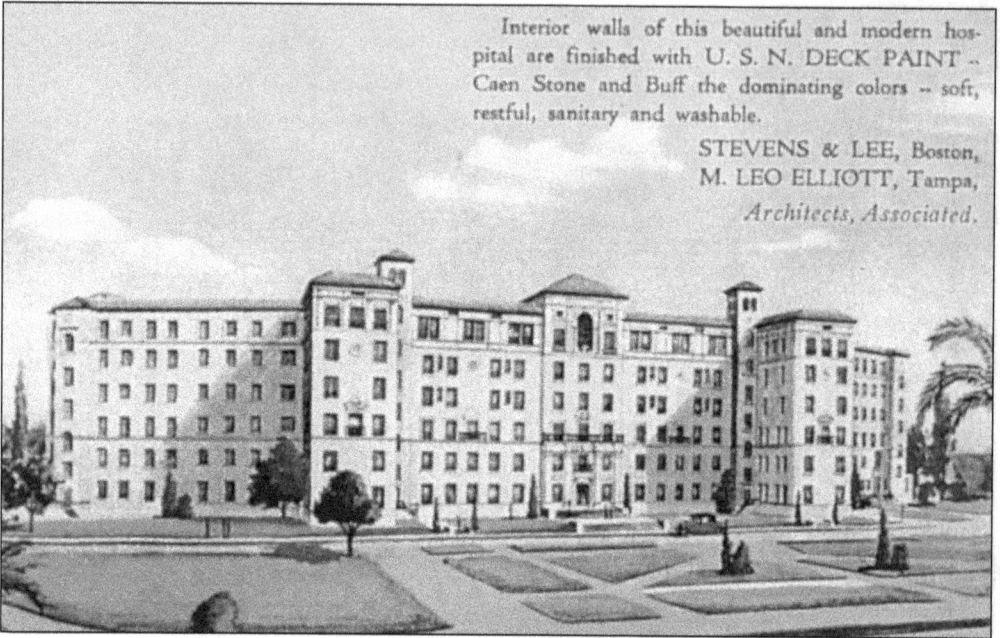

Interior walls of this beautiful and modern hospital are finished with U. S. N. DECK PAINT ~ Caen Stone and Buff the dominating colors ~ soft, restful, sanitary and washable.

STEVENS & LEE, Boston,
M. LEO ELLIOTT, Tampa,
Architects, Associated.

In 1925, developer D.P. Davis deeded land on which to build a hospital to the City of Tampa. A million-dollar bond issue followed and resulted in the building of the Tampa Municipal Hospital. The cost had exceeded that amount by over $300,000 by the time the hospital was completed in 1927.

The Gordon Keller Memorial Hospital was the first municipal hospital in Tampa and was named after Gordon Keller, a very prominent local philanthropist. Built in 1910 at 302 North Boulevard, the hospital cost $25,000 to build and had a total of 32 beds.

84

This modern plant was built in 1904, near Grand Central Avenue and the Hillsborough River. Later, it was named the Peter O. Knight Power House, and, by 1909, it served almost 3,500 customers. The plant has long been demolished, and *The Tampa Tribune* now occupies that location.

Waterworks on the Hillsborough River were developed after the artesian wells supplying Tampa were pushed to their limits. In 1923 this site was constructed, and A.W. Squires was appointed the first waterworks superintendent. The much-needed water replaced the hard water that came from the wells.

The Florida Brewing Company was located in southwest Ybor City, near Thirteenth Street and Fifth Avenue. The plant employed about 75 people with a payroll of just over $1,000 a week in 1912. The brewery was built in 1897, with money from the cigar manufacturers, at a cost of over $200,000.

This is the Port Tampa Gulf Refinery Works. Port Tampa is the deep-water terminal of the Florida West Coast Railroads. The refinery is very active in the refining of crude petroleum for local use and export. This c. 1910 picture shows the tank cars being loaded through the pipeline for processing.

Seven

SCHOOLS AND CHURCHES

Hillsborough County High School took care of all the educational needs of Tampa and surrounding areas in 1906 and was one of the finest schools in Florida at the time. It was located on the corner of Jefferson and Estelle Streets, north of the city. The two-story wooden structure cost a little over $5,000 to build.

Pictured here, c. 1908, is Michigan Avenue Grammar School at 301 East Michigan Avenue. It was built in 1907 and was the finest elementary school in Hillsborough County at the time.

This is a view of Michigan Avenue Grammar School, looking southeast, right after it was built in 1907. Today, both the names of the school and the avenue have been changed. The avenue has become Columbus Drive and the school has become Robert E. Lee.

Hyde Park School was used as a promotional project for Tampa in the early 1900s. On postcards, this picture was accompanied by the following text: "Tampa's school buildings are modern and indicative of the temper of the new South." Here are recruited the coming progressive citizens of "The Magic City of the Gulf."

This is the way Hyde Park School looked in 1913. It was the first brick schoolhouse in Tampa and was built in 1890. Located at 502 South Boulevard at DeLeon Street, the school was later renamed Gorrie to honor the Apalachicola, Florida, inventor of the first ice-making machine, Dr. John Gorrie.

Hillsborough County High School was built at the turn of the century. The school had a four-year curriculum and was equipped with science laboratories, a library, and a large auditorium with a seating capacity of 250.

This is Hillsborough High School at Highland and Euclid Avenues. Built in 1911 and taking up a whole city block, this modern masonry structure was three stories high and replaced the former wooden building. The $60,000 building was the most modern and best-equipped school in Florida at the time.

The Convent of the Holy Names, pictured c. 1907, was a large, three-story, brick building located on Twiggs Street between Morgan and Pierce Streets. It was erected in 1891 at a cost of about $25,000. This busy Catholic school had 18 nuns as teachers.

The Academy of the Holy Names, "Mira Mar," (Spanish for "overlooking water") is located on beautiful Bayshore Boulevard, facing Tampa Bay. This attractive Catholic facility cost approximately $250,000 and was built in 1928. It is an accredited day school that is still in operation today at 3319 Bayshore Boulevard.

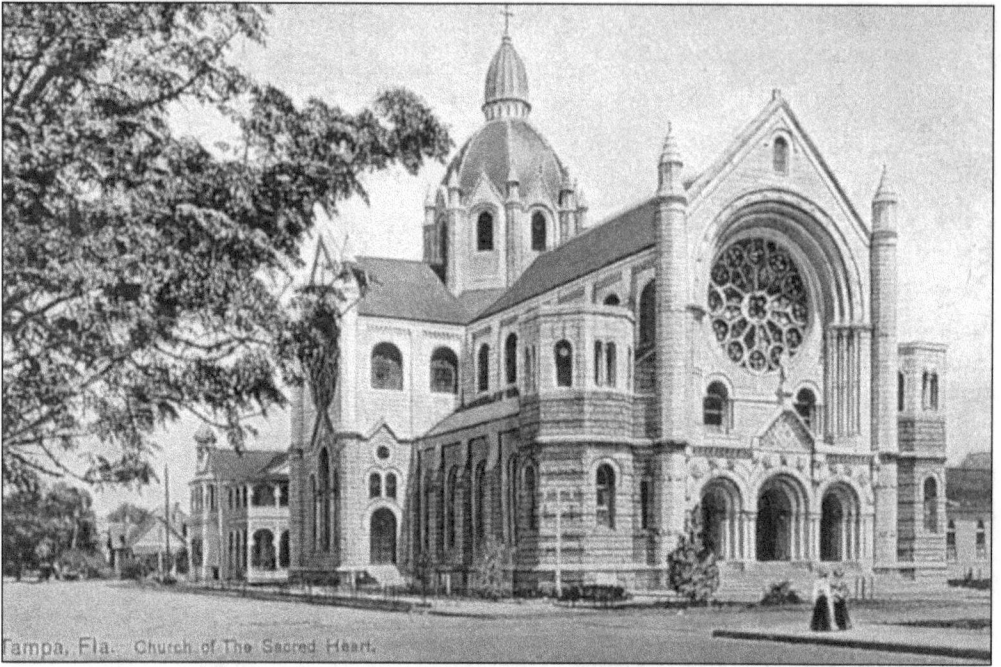

The Church of the Sacred Heart has often been acknowledged as the most beautiful Catholic church south of Washington, D.C. Dedicated in January 1905 by the bishop of St. Augustine, William Kenny, the church holds about 2,000 people and is located in downtown Tampa at Florida and Twiggs Streets.

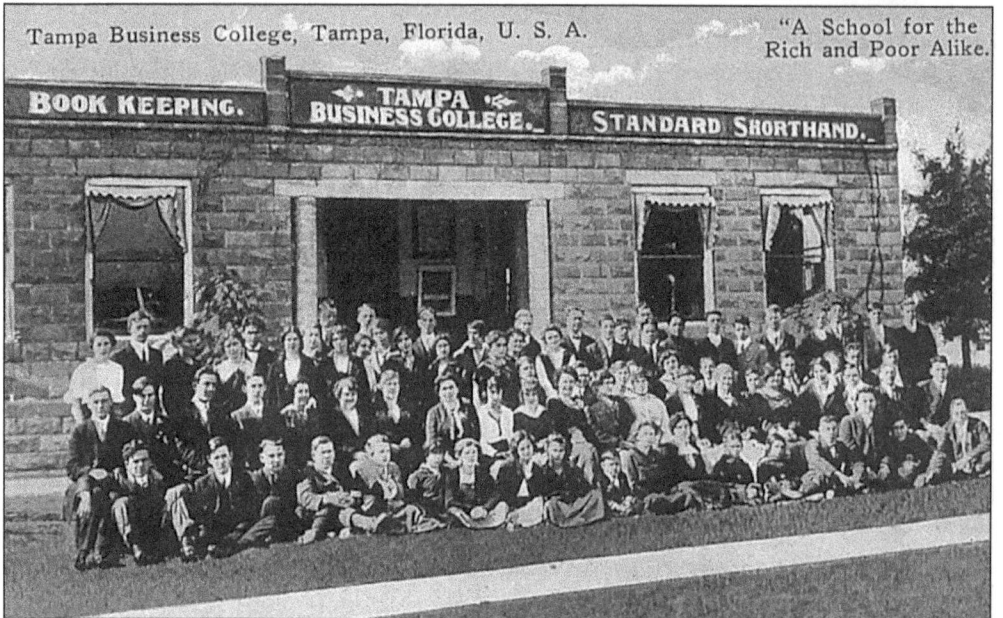

The Tampa Business College was located at Grand Central and Edison Avenues, only three blocks from The Tampa Bay Hotel. The college was established in 1890 and was open all year long. It was the most up-to-date business college in the South. L.M. Hatton was president at the time of this 1915 photo.

92

This is a rare view of the interior of Sacred Heart Church before it was furnished with pews, c. 1904. The altar cost $12,000 and was made of white marble. The altar rail cost another $5,000. Both were donated by two wealthy men from Philadelphia, in memory of their mother who died while visiting Tampa. The ladies of Sacred Heart Church donated hand-sewn items to be sold at regularly-held bazaars, which were headed by Rev. John Faulkes, to assist in the building fund as well.

One of the most beautiful sanctuaries of all the churches in Florida is right here in Tampa and it belongs to the Church of the Sacred Heart. Its fine marble altars and frescoed arches are truly a work of art.

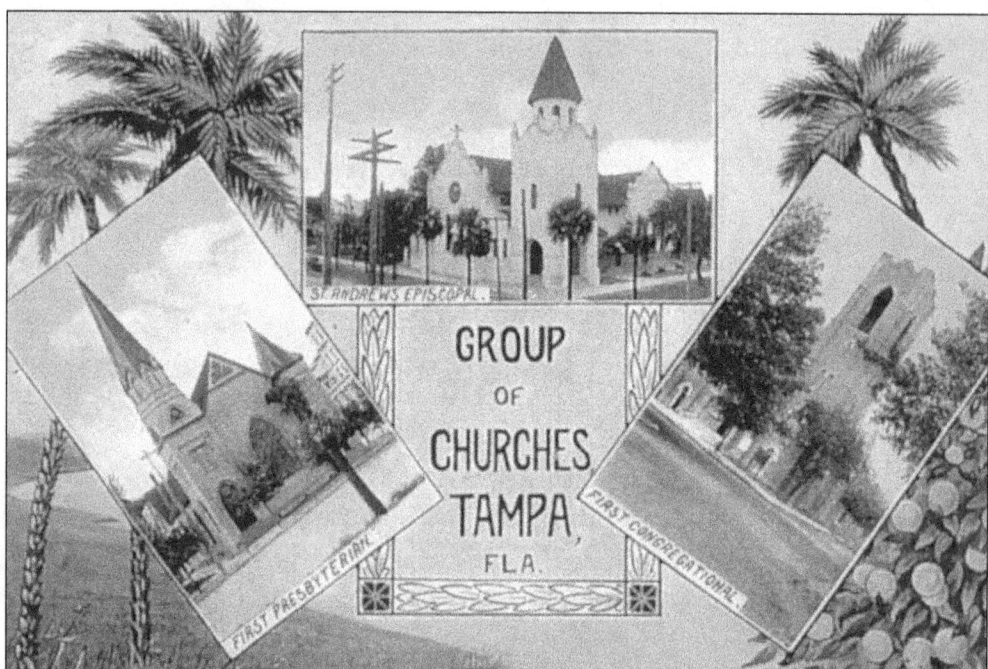

These are some of the principal churches in Tampa, c. 1915. These decorative pictures of churches were put on postcards to not only promote the churches but to promote the friendly city of Tampa as well. This card shows the various denominations available to residents and visitors.

These promotional postcards of 1915 were designed with orange trees, exotic palms, and a little art deco to add to the enticement of Tampa and to show that the city could accommodate a variety of religious denominations in beautiful houses of worship.

94

St. Andrews Episcopal Church is located at 505 Marion Street in downtown Tampa. In 1922, the church had a membership of 380. Its membership has continued to grow through the years and is now well over 800.

This is a beautiful view of the interior of St. Andrews Episcopal Church, c. 1915. The sanctuary was not air-conditioned at the time, but as you can see, there were plenty of hand fans available on the backs of the pews for cooling off during a hot sermon.

The First Presbyterian Church was located on the southeast corner of Florida Avenue and Zack Street. The DeSoto Hotel is across the street to the right and to the left, just out of sight, is the old Peninsular Telephone Company. This photo was taken *c*. 1907.

The First Congregational Church, located at 2201 Florida Avenue and East Francis Street, in the northern part of Tampa Heights, was constructed in 1906, and this photo was taken not long after that. The abandoned building is now being considered for renewal and preservation.

96

Hyde Park Methodist Church, located on the southwest corner of Platt Street and Cedar Avenue, was built in 1907 at a cost of $24,000. Another $6,000 was spent on furnishings. The cornerstone was laid by Bishop C.B. Galloway, and the church was dedicated by Bishop E.E. Hoss. Mrs. A.C. Clewis was the chairperson of the building committee.

The First Baptist Church is located at Lafayette Street and Hyde Park Avenue, west of downtown Tampa and south of the Tampa Bay Hotel. This red brick church was a welcomed addition to the many churches in the Hyde Park area. This photo was taken c. 1908.

The First Christian Church, located at 350 Hyde Park Avenue, was built at a cost of $250,000 (which included the property) in 1922. The Church's membership was 360 then and growing fast. The large brick building's architect was R.H. Hunt Company.

St. Paul's Methodist Church was in downtown Tampa, at 1101 Marion Street. This view is c. 1914. This beautiful church's steeple was so high that it could be seen from anywhere in Tampa. The church was demolished in the late 1960s.

Eight

LEISURE TIME

This was an advertising postcard for the Florida State Fair held February 16-21, 1916. The annual fair brought tourists and people from all over Florida to Tampa. The fair had rides, races, county exhibits, and livestock competitions as well as many agricultural displays of Florida's abundant citrus and produce.

The Florida State Fairgrounds were located northwest of the Tampa Bay Hotel grounds in order to accommodate and promote H.B. Plant's huge hotel. A large race track for horses was an enormous draw, as were the midway, games, and many exhibits.

King Gasparilla VIII is shown receiving the keys to the city of Tampa in 1914 from the Honorable Donald B. McKay, who was the mayor of Tampa for 14 years (1910–1920 and 1928–1932). McKay was also the writer of a column on Florida history called "Pioneer Florida," which was featured in the Sunday *Tampa Tribune* for many years.

This 1914 Gasparilla Invasion had plenty of pirates and Indians trying to gain control of the city. This part of the celebration came with tepees, dances, and parades.

This Gasparilla float , c. 1914, represents the Hillsborough County Humane Society. The float not only had animals pulling it, it had live animals riding on it. The sign on the horse says, "Water Frequently."

One of the many musical floats of the 1914 Gasparilla Parade was manned by a mutual aid society from Ybor City. This float is shown on Lafayette Street, near Plant Park. The floats at this time were all pulled by animals.

The Gasparilla flotilla of 1914 includes the *Gasparilla VII*. This view shows the area between the Tampa Bay Hotel grounds and the Atlantic Coast Line warehouse area in downtown Tampa. In the background, on the right, is the Bay View Hotel.

The 1915 Florida State Fair and Gasparilla Parade were held February 12-16, 1915. The Shriners are cutting up in true festive fashion at the fair's grandstand. What's really in those bottles?

Participating in the Gasparilla Parade in downtown Tampa, c. 1919, the Oscar Daniels Company float, "Tampa," is shown in front of the Economical Drug Store at 817 Franklin Street. The shipbuilding company contracted with the U.S. Navy to build ten 10,000-ton ships over a six-year period during which the company employed 3,400 people at peak production. After six years of construction, the Tampa Ship and Engineering Company took over all future contracts.

This is the boat landing at Sulphur Springs. Regular daily excursion boats ran from downtown Tampa to this area and streetcar lines connected the very popular recreational facility to other parts of Tampa.

Sulphur Springs is located about 6 miles north of Tampa, on the Hillsborough River. The spring has an 8-foot wall surrounding it and a flow of 30,000 gallons per minute. The average water temperature is 76 degrees. Immediately adjacent to the spring were a pavilion, boating facilities, an alligator farm, and an amusement park.

Sulphur Springs, Tampa, Fla.

This is a close-up view of the Sulphur Springs pool. Many people have come to enjoy the famous "Stomawa" mineral water found here. "Stomawa" is the Seminole word for stomach water and was said to be extremely healthy to drink. People came from miles around to enjoy its many benefits.

Swimming Pool, Sulphur Springs, Tampa, Fla.

The water in Sulphur Springs pool is claimed to have the same benefits as the water in the famed Kissingen Springs in Germany. People have visited Sulphur Springs from all over the world for health as well as recreational reasons. The spring was adjoined by a park that featured boating, dancing, and picnic facilities.

The Casino. Ballast Point. Near Tampa, Fla.

This is a view from Tampa Bay, looking toward Ballast Point Park in South Tampa, with the large docking facilities and walkway visible. Fishing, boating, and swimming could be enjoyed by all. The park was located only 4 miles south of downtown Tampa.

ENTRANCE TO BALLAST POINT PARK TAMPA, FLA.   1797

This is the streetcar landing station at the entrance to Ballast Point Park in South Tampa. The streetcars of the early 1900s had a regular run from downtown Tampa to Ballast Point Park and Pier along the shores of Tampa Bay.

Section of the Board Walk, Ballast Point, Tampa, Fla.

Ballast Point was one of Tampa's most popular amusement parks in the early 1900s. The boardwalk was lighted in the evenings for recreational use. The park was formerly owned by Tampa Electric, who donated it to the city of Tampa.

The Poinciana Theatre, seen here *c.* 1913, was located on Florida Avenue and the southwest corner of Cass Street in downtown Tampa. It was advertised as the most attractive and coolest theatre in the South. Photoplays, which were accompanied by a fine orchestra, changed daily for constant entertainment. W.L. Hill was the manager at the time of this photo.

This is the end of the line for the Seventh Avenue streetcar's run to Palmetto Beach, just south of Ybor City. The streetcar seen here is in DeSoto Park in the northern section of Palmetto Beach, bordered by Ybor City to the north and Sparkman Bay to the south.

In 1907, Palmetto Beach was a picturesque peninsula along the shores of Sparkman Bay, near the city limits. The sandy beach is skirted by lofty palmettos. The Marconi Wireless Station was located here, along with boating facilities and a pier.

DeSoto Park was a very popular recreational area serviced by streetcars and small boats. At the time of this picture, Tampa Electric owned the entire park. They later donated the land to the city of Tampa. In 1919, it became a popular spot for "Tin Can" tourists (people who traveled by automobile) from all over the country.

Bathing in Gulf near Tampa, Fla.

One of the many beaches along the coastline of the Tampa Bay area is seen here, c. 1910. The latest fashion of the day is shown here by the young and old alike.

Palmaceia Springs is about 3 miles south of downtown Tampa, near Tampa Bay and just off Bayshore Boulevard. The spring was known for its high mineral content and health benefits. This picture was taken *c*. 1905.

This view of Palmaceia Springs shows the discharge that flows into Tampa Bay, *c*. 1908. The streetcar line that runs to Port Tampa and Ballast Point makes a regular stop here. Thomas Palmer owned this popular swimming pool.

In this c. 1907 image is the canal leading to Tampa Bay from Palmaceia Springs. It travels from the spring's discharge to the bay under Bayshore Boulevard by way of a large culvert.

Going Crabbing. When the Crab gets out of the basket. Tampa Bay, Fla.

Fishing was not the only pursuit that Tampa Bay was known for in 1910. All forms of sea life were plentiful and easy to catch.

Out for a good time in 1910 on a beautiful day, by a beautiful bay, two beautiful young ladies enjoy a typical Sunday afternoon in Tampa.

Many pleasurable days were spent sailing for enjoyment on Tampa Bay. This risqué, c. 1913 view does not go unnoticed by a casual observer.

112

Nine

CLUBS AND
ORGANIZATIONS

One of the oldest social clubs in Tampa, the beautiful Tampa Yacht and Country Club cost $20,000 to build. It adjoins Ballast Point Park and Tampa Bay on Bayshore Boulevard, and had its own private dock and pier that could be reached by the Port Tampa streetcar line.

Hillsborough Lodge Home, Tampa, Fla.

This Hillsborough Lodge Home was located on the northwest corner of Lafayette and Morgan Streets. The grounds were abundant, with beautiful tropical foliage. Meetings were held here on the second and fourth Tuesday of each month. This c. 1916 view shows the third building constructed since the lodge was founded in Tampa January 24, 1850. The building has since been replaced by a masonry building.

Tampa Automobile and Golf Club, Tampa, Fla.

The Tampa Automobile Club was organized in 1906, when little more than 100 autos were known to be in the Tampa Bay area. Members would tour as far away as Clearwater and Tarpon Springs. In 1909, the group sponsored a "cross-country" race to Jacksonville and back to promote the need for better roads. The participants averaged 10 miles per hour, went 543 miles, and took 4 days.

The Elks Club was located at the corner of Florida Avenue and Madison Street, just opposite the county courthouse. The popular and prosperous club was once a private frame-house residence. It was purchased in 1905 and remodeled at a cost of $17,000.

This beautiful Elks Club House replaced the earlier wood-frame one. The red-brick building trimmed in marble is Lodge #708. The structure cost about $125,000 in 1913 and was the old homestead of Dr. John P. Wall.

The YMCA was organized in Tampa on August 21, 1907. This five-story building is located downtown, on Florida Avenue and Zack Street. It was built in 1908. William Jennings Bryan helped dedicate the building.

This Knights of Pythian Castle was built on the southwest corner of Lafayette and Morgan Streets in 1913 on the old homestead of John T. Givens. The organization's members enjoyed the privileges of billiards, social halls, and various functions throughout the year. This photo was taken c. 1918.

The German-American Club was located on Nebraska and Eleventh Avenues, in the extreme western part of Ybor City where Tampa Heights begins. The inset is the president of the club, George Stecher. The German influence in Tampa was strong, but when World War I came along, that influence was greatly neutralized.

Centro Espanol in Ybor City is located at 1536 Seventh Avenue. This large building is used for social recreation and entertainment by the Hispanic community and is one of the most active in Tampa. Many concerts and balls are held in this majestic facility.

The Centro Asturiano Club House was located at Nebraska and Ninth Avenues in Ybor City. Considered to be one of the most beautiful buildings in the city, it was dedicated in 1909 but was destroyed by fire in 1912 and replaced by the structure that still stands at Nebraska and Palm Avenues.

The newer Centro Asturiano building is located at Nebraska and Palm Avenues and has a gym, a library, and a huge auditorium used for theatrical entertainment. The furnishings and building cost about $140,000.

This beautiful, two-story wooden clubhouse, Centro Espanol, was located on Seventh Avenue and Sixteenth Street. Its members enjoyed the benefits of their own health care system, which provided not only hospital care but day-to-day care from physicians for a nominal fee.

This Spanish Casino is known as Centro Espanol of West Tampa and is located on the corner of Howard Avenue and Cherry Street in West Tampa. Its members met for social events, music, and sports. One of the largest Hispanic clubs in Tampa, it is currently undergoing restoration.

The Cuban Club, first organized in 1900, is located at 2010 Avenue Republica de Cuba North. The club provided health care for the members as well as a gathering place for its members to talk, smoke, and drink Cuban coffee. After a hard day's work, many of the local cigar workers would gather there to unwind.

The first Italian Club, founded in 1894, was located at Seventh Avenue in Ybor City between Seventeenth and Eighteenth Streets in 1912 and was destroyed by fire in 1915. In 1917, the Italian Club built a new facility at Seventh Avenue and Eighteenth Street that still stands today. The cost of the new clubhouse was $95,000 (including furnishings) and had about 1,000 members in 1917.

Ten

WEST TAMPA
AND YBOR CITY

This is Main Street in West Tampa. Notice the Florida Brewery Company on the left. Tampa's rapid growth from the many cigar factories caused a sprawl east and west. In 1910, the suburb of West Tampa was a flourishing Cuban and Spanish community with a strong economy and about a hundred cigar factories, large and small.

These are Spanish and Cuban tenement houses. The government census of 1903 recorded 141 tobacco manufacturers in the Tampa area. Over 5,000 people were employed in the making of Havana leaf cigars. About half of that number lived in the West Tampa area.

The A. Santaella & Company Cigar Factory is located at 1507 North Armenia Avenue in West Tampa. At one time, it was the largest cigar factory in the world. This 1908 view is looking east.

At one time, Cuesta, Rey, & Company, located at 2015 North Howard Avenue in West Tampa, was the largest independent clear Havana cigar factory in the world. They advertised their product as being "For Gentlemen of Fastidious Taste" and "purveyors of Havana cigars to the royal court of Spain." This image was made c. 1908.

The J.W. Roberts & Son Cigar Factory was located in West Tampa at 1322 Garcia Avenue. The building took up a whole block and had 25,000 square feet of floor space. No machinery was found within its walls. All cigars were hand made by Cuban workmen exactly as they would be made in Cuba. The company was the largest "direct to the consumer" Havana cigar business in the world.

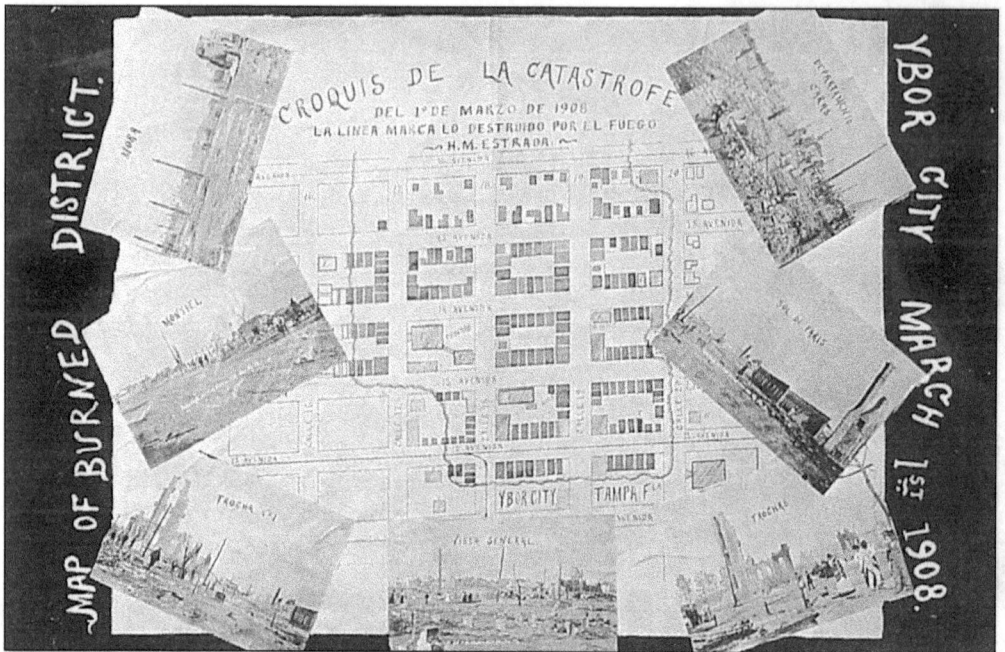

MAP OF BURNED DISTRICT.

CROQUIS DE LA CATASTROFE
DEL 1° DE MARZO DE 1908
LA LINEA MARCA LO DESTRUIDO POR EL FUEGO
~ H.M. ESTRADA. ~

YBOR CITY MARCH 1ST 1908.

This is a multi-view of the devastation that occurred on March 1, 1908. This fire spread from Sixteenth Avenue to beyond Twelfth Avenue and from Twentieth Street to almost Sixteenth Street. The fire almost burned the entire Ybor City to the ground.

This photo shows some of the survivors of the Ybor City fire of March 1908. The fire burned more than 350 homes as well as many commercial structures and cigar factories like the one shown here.

124

This is Seventh Avenue looking west, c. 1907. On the left is the Ybor City Post Office; on the right is the old Centro Espanol Club House at the intersection of Sixteenth Street. The bilingual sign at the post office reflects the local heritage.

Ybor City's Seventh Avenue is pictured here, looking west. The large building on the right is the Eden Theater, located between Sixteenth and Seventeenth Streets. Later, the Eden was replaced by the Kress 5 & 10¢ store. There were as many residences on Seventh Avenue as there were businesses when this picture was taken in 1907.

This is Ybor City's main street, Seventh Avenue, c. 1908. The cigar industry brought thousands of immigrant workers to the area from around the world. The Hispanic suburb of Tampa was a self-contained community with a flavor all its own. The retail shops to the left are Ybor Furniture and Metropolitan Drug Store; on the right is the La Casa Blanca hotel and restaurant.

This bird's-eye view of Ybor City shows La Casa Blanca hotel and restaurant on the right, c. 1907. Several cigar factories can be seen as well, and in the foreground are the bricks to be used for improving the dirt streets.

Looking west on Seventh Avenue in Ybor City, c. 1915, is Centro Espanol Club-(right). Located at 536 Seventh Avenue, the club provided regular theatrical attractions, as shown on the marquee in front. This predominately Hispanic community was just a brief streetcar ride from downtown Tampa.

This c. 1915 scene in a residential area of Ybor City was probably taken on a Sunday afternoon. At the time, the white buildings on the right were the most modern structures and not the typical residence of the inhabitants of Ybor City. The concrete homes were built by Sanchez & Haya and located on Fourteenth Street and Tenth Avenue.

Shown here, c. 1908, is the Cherokee Club on the corner of Ninth Avenue and Fourteenth Street. The building housed a restaurant, a hotel, and at one time, the Ybor City Chamber of Commerce. The building was called the Cherokee Club before the name was changed the present-day El Pasaje.

This c. 1909 view shows Seventh Avenue, looking east. On the left is a grocery delivery wagon and the old Centro Espanol Club. The intersection at the streetcar is Seventh Avenue and Sixteenth Street. All of these wooden structures have been replaced by red-brick buildings.

www.ingramcontent.com/pod-product-compliance
Lightning Source LLC
Chambersburg PA
CBHW080909100426
42812CB00007B/2216